Strategize
Execute
and
Dominate

A practical Guide to Winning Big in Business

Adedayo Adetokun

Preface

A Compass for Business Voyagers

In the turbulent waters of the current business landscape, survival is insufficient. We, the intrepid captains of our commercial ships, crave not just safe harbors but uncharted islands of dominance.

This book, Strategize, Execute, and Dominate: A Practical Guide to Winning Big in Business, is your compass for this magnificent quest. It is not a dusty tome of stale formulas, but a map crafted with the ink of experience and the fire of innovation.

Forget the siren song of shortcuts and quick fixes. This voyage demands strategic discipline – a commitment to understanding your market, aligning your vision with reality, and crafting a unique value proposition that slices through noise. You will learn to wield the power of disruptive innovation, not as a fleeting trend but as a guiding principle for building a moat around your business, a barrier against the tides of mediocrity.

However, a strategy without execution is one in which a ship is lost at sea. This book is equipped with tools to transform your vision into action, with chapters dedicated to building high-performing teams, streamlining operations for optimal efficiency, and navigating financial currents with the wisdom of seasoned navigators.

However, dominance is not a solo endeavor. It is a symphony where every member of the team plays a vital note. You will discover the qualities of the indelible leader, who inspires, empowers, and leaves a legacy in the hearts and minds of those they guide.

This journey is not only about conquering markets and shattering sales records. It is about building a sustainable enterprise that thrives in harmony with its people and planet. You will learn to integrate ESG principles into the fabric of your business, leaving a legacy of positive impact that resonates far beyond the bottom line.

So, open this book, brave voyager, and let it be your guide. Chart your course, set your sails, and embark on an exhilarating journey towards business mastery. The future is not a destination; it is a canvas waiting for your brushstroke.

Strategize, execute, and dominate, and leave your mark around the world.

Table of Contents

Introduction

From Aspiring Strategist to Business Maverick

Forget dusty boardrooms and jargon-laden textbooks. This book does not address dry theories or academic exercises. It is about igniting your inner strategist and unleashing the raw power of strategic thinking to conquer the business battlefield.

Are you tired of playing defense? Tired of reacting to market shifts and chasing the latest trends? Do you yearn for a blueprint for dominance, a roadmap to carve your own path, and leave your competitors gasping in your dust?

Thus, welcome the revolution.

"Strategize, Execute, and Dominate" is your passport to a world where vision becomes reality, and ambition translates into action.

We will tear down the walls of conventional thinking and equip you with weapons of strategic warfare:

- o **Strategic canvas:** Learn to paint your masterpiece, aligning your vision, mission, and values with the canvas of your market reality.
- o **The art of the competitive edge:** Go beyond differentiation and discover unconventional strategies that leave your rivals scrambling for their footing.

- Building **high-performance teams:** Cultivate a culture of strategic agility where people become an unstoppable force, executing their vision with a laser-like focus.

- **Market intelligence:** Uncover the secrets of customers, understand their deepest desires, and craft marketing campaigns that resonate.

- **Innovation imperative:** Embrace the future, harness the power of disruptive technologies, and turn ideas into game-changing products and services.

- This is not just a book; it is also a strategic manifesto. We will challenge your assumptions, ignite your passion, and guide you through the transformative power of strategic thinking. You will learn to:

- **Navigate uncertainty:** Turn chaos into opportunity, adapt to lightning speed, and emerge from every crisis stronger than before.

- **Embrace sustainable growth:** Build a legacy that extends beyond profits, a legacy of social responsibility, and a positive impact on the world.

- **Leave your mark:** Become a leader worth following, an inspiration for your team, and a force to be reckoned with in your industry.

Are you ready to shed the shackles of mediocrity and claim your rightful place as a business maverick?

This is your journey. This is your victory…..Let us begin!!!

Chapter One

Strategy Imperative: Why Strategy Matters More than Ever.

In the realm of modern business, adaptation is not just a choice; it is also a necessity. This chapter lays the groundwork for understanding the pivotal role of strategic thinking in today's rapidly evolving landscape.

This chapter serves as a beacon illuminating the transformative power of strategic thought amidst the shifting currents of technology, globalization, and consumer behavior. It ventures beyond conventional wisdom, debunking myths that often shroud the concept of strategy while guiding readers toward a profound understanding of its true essence.

At its core, this chapter is a roadmap for businesses seeking not only survival but also the ascent to thrive in an intensely competitive arena. It urges a departure from mere reactionary measures towards an initiative-taking and visionary approach, where defining ambition becomes the cornerstone for strategic success.

Join this exploration as we delve into the dynamic interplay between strategy and success, uncovering the imperative nature of strategic thinking in today's business world.

The Changing Business Landscape and the Critical Role of Strategic Thinking

The contemporary business landscape is characterized by unprecedented volatility, uncertainty, complexity, and ambiguity (VUCA). Rapid technological advancements, globalization, changing consumer behaviors, and sociopolitical shifts have contributed to this dynamic environment. Strategic thinking has become paramount in navigating and thriving amidst these changes.

a. **Adapting to Change:** Businesses must continuously adapt to stay relevant. Strategic thinking involves anticipating shifts, identifying opportunities, and mitigating risks before escalation.

b. **Competitive Advantage:** Strategic thinking helps foster sustainable competitive advantage by leveraging strengths and exploring innovative avenues. This involves evaluating market dynamics and understanding customer needs to effectively differentiate oneself.

c. **Flexibility and Resilience:** Strategic thinking fosters a culture of flexibility and resilience. Companies that adopt a strategic approach can pivot swiftly when faced with unforeseen challenges, thereby ensuring continuity and growth.

Debunking Myths About Strategy and Overcoming Common Misconceptions

a. **Strategy is Only for Top Management:** Contrary to popular beliefs, strategy should be inclusive, involving employees at all levels. It is about aligning everyone is efforts with shared goals.

b. **Strategy Equals Planning:** While planning is a component, strategy involves more than just the outlining steps. It concerns making informed decisions based on analysis, foresight, and adaptability.

c. **Once created, Strategy Is Set in Stone:** Effective strategy is dynamic. Constant evaluation, adjustments, and flexibility are required to respond to evolving circumstances.

d. **Execution Trumps Strategy:** Execution is crucial, but without a sound strategy, efforts can be misdirected. The strategy guides execution by setting a clear direction.

e. **Short-term focus is sufficient:** Long-term thinking is essential for sustainability. Short-term gains should align with broader strategic goals.

Defining Your Ambition: From Surviving to Thriving in the Competitive Arena

    a. **Vision and Mission:** Defining a clear vision and mission is fundamental. A vision outlines the future state, while the mission defines the purpose and values that guide the organization.

    b. **Setting Ambitious Goals:** Moving beyond mere survival means setting ambitious, yet achievable goals. These goals inspire and drive organizations towards growth and innovation.

    c. **Strategic Prioritization:** Not all goals are equal. Strategic thinking involves prioritizing objectives, allocating resources, and focusing on areas that align with overarching strategies.

    d. **Continuous Improvement:** Thriving in a competitive arena requires a culture of continuous improvement. Companies must learn from their experiences, adapt, and innovate to stay ahead.

The current business environment needs a strategic mindset to navigate uncertainties, seize opportunities, and foster sustainable growth. Embracing strategic thinking at all levels of an organization and debunking common misconceptions are pivotal steps towards achieving long-term success and thriving in competition.

Why Strategy Matters…

Case Study: Strategic Thinking in a Dynamic Business Landscape

Background: 4ace Corporation, a mid-sized tech company, grappled with industry disruptions, market fluctuations, and intensifying competition. To fortify its position in an ever-evolving landscape, the leadership embarked on strategic transformation, aiming not only to survive but also to thrive.

Phase 1: Adapting to Change

The company identified the shifting dynamics within the tech sector: rapid advancements in AI, changing consumer preferences, and emerging market entrants. By embracing strategic thinking, the 4ace Corporation initiated a proactive stance. They have established dedicated task forces to forecast trends, anticipate industry shifts, and align their strategies accordingly.

Result: Anticipating the rise of AI-driven solutions, 4ace Corporation strategically redirected R&D efforts and swiftly launched innovative AI-powered products that met emerging market demands. This adaptability not only maintained their relevance, but also positioned them as pioneers in a burgeoning tech niche.

Phase 2: Debunking Myths About Strategy

Recognizing the common misconceptions surrounding strategy, the 4ace Corporation initiated a comprehensive change-management program. They instilled a cultural shift, emphasizing that strategic thinking was not solely confined to the upper echelons but was integral at all levels.

Results: Employees across departments were encouraged to contribute ideas and align their daily efforts with the company's strategic direction.

The misconception that strategy equals rigid planning was dismantled, emphasizing that adaptability and continuous evaluation were critical.

Phase 3: Defining Ambition Beyond Survival

The 4ace Corporation revamped its mission and vision, aligning them with ambitious, yet achievable goals. They emphasized not just surviving but thriving by fostering a culture of innovation and continual improvement.

Results: Clear strategic prioritization aided in the effective allocation of resources. The company streamlined its operations by focusing on projects aligned with its overarching strategy. This shift has led to enhanced productivity, increased employee morale, and a more cohesive, purposeful workforce.

Conclusion: Through strategic thinking, the 4ace Corporation transformed its outlook from reactive survival to proactive excellence. By adapting to industry changes, dispelling misconceptions, and setting ambitious, yet focused goals, they became resilient to market fluctuations. Their journey from embracing strategic thinking to thriving in a competitive arena serves as a beacon for organizations seeking sustained success in a dynamic business landscape.

This case study exemplifies the transformative power of strategic thinking, guiding the 4ace Corporation to navigate uncertainties, seize opportunities, and foster sustainable growth, setting a benchmark for strategic agility and success in the contemporary business world.

Chapter Two
The Strategic Canvas: Build Your Winning Formula

The strategic canvas!!!.... Sounds impressive, doesn't it? Like a masterpiece, you will hang in the boardroom, baffling visitors with its cryptic symbols and indecipherable scribbles. But fear not, for behind the fancy terminology lies a simple truth: your strategic canvas is a glorified tablecloth for your business dreams.

Think of it as a gourmet picnic. You would not just toss your charcuterie and artisanal cheeses on a bare table? Would you? No, you would need a vibrant, colorful spread to highlight your culinary artistry. Similarly, your strategic canvas is where you arrange the delectable ingredients of your business vision: your mission, values, goals, and juicy market analysis you spent hours drooling over.

Now, some people might tell you that this is a serious business. They will whisper about SWOT analyses, competitor audits, and strategic positioning like it is some sacred incantation. However, let me tell you, a good strategic canvas should have a dash of humor, a sprinkle of self-awareness, and even a dollop of ridiculousness (think unicorn-themed marketing for a stodgy accounting firm).

Why the fun and games, you ask? A playful approach keeps things fresh, sparks creativity, and prevents you from being bogged down in jargon-infested swamps. Moreover, who wants to work with a business that takes itself too seriously? We are all just glorified circus performers trying to juggle deadlines, budgets, and existential dread – might as well laugh at its absurdity!

So, grab your metaphorical picnic basket, let us spread out that tablecloth, and get ready to paint your masterpiece. We will explore the essential elements of your canvas, from the juicy mission statement that should make your employees weep with pride (or at least stop complaining about coffee) to the market analysis that reveals your competitors' biggest weaknesses.

The strategic canvas, far from being mere decorative elements, serves as the cornerstone of a well-defined and actionable business strategy. It is the artist's palette, the architect's blueprint, and the navigator's map – a visual representation of your aspirations–translated into tangible elements that guide every move. Unlike the dusty, static documents of the past, this canvas pulsates with the dynamic reality of your market and the ever-evolving aspirations of your organization.

At its core, the strategic canvas rests on four pillars.

1. **Vision:** The audacious, aspirational statement that paints a picture of the ideal future. It is not a destination but a North Star, guiding your decisions and rallying your team. Think of it as the summit you strive to conquer, the Everest of your business ambitions.

2. **Mission:** The concrete expression of your vision, the "how" behind the "what." It defines your core purpose, reason you exist, and value you bring to the world. A well-crafted mission statement should be clear, concise, and resonate with every member of the organization, from the C-suite to the intern-making coffee.

3. **Values:** The guiding principles that underpin every action, the bedrock of your ethical and operational framework. Values such as integrity, innovation, and customer focus become the compass that steers you through choppy waters of uncertainty and ethical dilemmas.

4. **Market Share Analysis:** The vital intelligence report maps the landscape that you navigate. It is a comprehensive assessment of your industry, competitors, target audience, and the opportunities and threats that lie ahead. This analysis should be data-driven, insightful, and constantly evolving to reflect ever-changing market dynamics.

Now, let us delve deeper into each pillar and explore how they weave together to form your strategic masterpiece.

Vision	Mission	Values	Market Share Analysis
o Craft with clarity: Avoid ambiguity and vagueness. Your vision should be a vivid picture, a tangible destination that inspires and motivates. o Think big, but stay grounded: Dream audaciously, but anchor your vision and market feasibility. o Keep it relevant: Your vision should evolve with the market and your organization's capabilities.	o Focus on impact: Define your unique contribution to the world, the positive ripple effects your business creates. o Make it actionable: Translate your mission into concrete goals and objectives, turning aspirations into achievable milestones. o Embrace ownership: Every member of your team should understand and champion the mission, making it their own.	o Live by your principles: Do not just preach your values, live them. Let them permeate your organizational culture and guide every decision you make. o Align with your vision: Values should be the bridge between your aspirations and your actions, ensuring your journey remains true to your north star. o Be authentic and transparent: Do not shy away from displaying your values, even if they differ from industry norms.	o Gather the right data: Go beyond superficial trends and dig deep into customer insights, competitor strategies, and industry forecasts. o Identify key trends and disruptors: Understand the emerging forces that could reshape your market and anticipate their impact on your business. o Embrace continuous learning: The market is a living organism, and your analysis should evolve alongside it.

Recall that the strategic canvas is not a static document to be admired from afar. It is a living, breathing roadmap that constantly evolves as one learns, adapts, and grows. Use it to make strategic decisions, track your progress, and hold yourself accountable for your journey towards your vision.

So, grab your metaphorical paintbrush and begin crafting your masterpiece. Let your vision guide your strokes, your mission fuel your passion, your values be the guiding lines, and your market analysis inform every color choice. This is your canvas, story, and strategic legacy.

This is where the art of strategy truly comes alive.

Visualize this...

Imagine you are a fledgling coffee shop, nestled in the heart of a bustling city. Your vision is to become the city's "cozy haven for caffeine connoisseurs," a place where people linger over aromatic brews, connect with friends, and escape the daily grind. Your mission is to "cultivate a community of coffee enthusiasts through ethically sourced beans, handcrafted artistry, and warm hospitality." Your values emphasize sustainability, fair trade practices, and fostering a welcoming environment for everyone.

Now it is time to paint your market analysis onto the canvas. You discover that your target audience craves high-quality coffee experiences beyond the typical chain shops. They appreciate locally sourced ingredients, unique brewing methods, and a commitment to sustainability. However, competition is fierce, with established cafes and trendy pop-ups vying for attention.

Armed with this knowledge, you craft your strategies:

Focus on niche offerings: Instead of competing head-on with mass-market chains, you specialize in single-origin beans, pour-over techniques, and cold brew variations.

Partner with local roasters: This ensures ethically sourced beans and supports the community while offering unique flavors.

Create a cozy atmosphere: Comfortable seating, warm lighting, and curated playlists foster a welcoming space for lingering and conversation.

Embrace technology: Offer online ordering, loyalty programs, and educational coffee workshops to engage customers and build a community.

By meticulously aligning your vision, mission, values, and market analysis, your strategic canvas becomes a blueprint for success.

Chapter Three
Identify Your Competitive Edge: Beyond Differentiation

Forget the tiring clichés of "blue oceans" and "unique selling propositions." Current business battlefield, differentiation alone is a flimsy shield against the relentless onslaught of competition. This battlefield demands a weapon forged in the fires of strategic ingenuity, a competitive edge so sharp it severs the throats of rivals and leaves one standing tall on the victor's podium.

This is not about slapping a trendy label on one's product or tweaking the logo to look oh-so-slightly different. It is about diving deep into the DNA of your organization, uncovering the hidden strengths and unique capabilities that make one tick. It is about mining the depths of customer understanding, uncovering their unspoken desires and crafting experiences that resonate with their very souls.

This is a call to arms for the strategists, the innovators, the relentless pursuers of excellence. We will rip apart the tired frameworks of "me-too" marketing and expose the secrets of building an unbreakable competitive edge. We will explore the avenues that lead you beyond mere differentiation, into a realm where dominance is not a dream, but a tangible reality.

…get ready!!!

Unmask the hidden gems within the organization – those unique strengths that set the organization apart like a diamond in a field of pebbles.

Delve into the minds and hearts of the customers – discover what truly makes them tick and craft experiences that leave them breathless.

Light the fire of innovation – embrace unconventional thinking and unleash the disruptive forces that will rewrite the rules of your industry.

Forge a moat of operational excellence – streamline processes, leverage technology, and build an organization that runs like a well-oiled machine.

Erect barriers built on sustainability – integrate ethical and environmental principles into core strategy, attracting consumers who value purpose as much as profit.

This is not a spectator sport. This is a journey of self-discovery, a quest for the competitive edge that will propel one to the top of the food chain. So, grab your metaphorical sword and shield, and prepare to embark on a strategic odyssey that will leave your competitors gasping for air in your dust.

In the intricate dance of competition, grasping your unique competitive edge extends beyond mere differentiation. Let us delve deeper into the essence of establishing a firm foothold amidst the competitive landscape.

Understand the Competitive Landscape and Identify Unique Value Proposition

Navigating the competitive terrain necessitates a profound comprehension of the market's intricacies. It is not just about standing out but understanding how and why. Begin by conducting comprehensive market research, analyzing consumer behaviors, and dissecting competitor strategies. Identify unmet needs or pain points in the market, allowing you to carve a niche that resonates uniquely with your audience. Emphasize the distinctive value your product or service brings—something that competitors struggle to replicate.

Exploit Disruptive Innovations and Embrace Unconventional Approaches

Thriving in a dynamic market requires not only adapting to change but also driving it. Dive into emerging trends, disruptive technologies, and innovative business models. Embrace a mindset of experimentation, encouraging teams to challenge conventional norms. Encourage cross-disciplinary collaboration to spark creativity and ingenuity. Seek to create breakthroughs or unconventional solutions that redefine industry norms, setting your brand apart as an innovator and trailblazer.

Build a Moat Around Your Business: Create Sustainable Competitive Advantages

Crafting a lasting competitive advantage involves constructing a fortress around your business. Invest in intellectual property, proprietary technology, or unique processes that become integral to your operations. Focus on building brand equity, customer loyalty, or a robust ecosystem around your product or service. Establish strategic partnerships or exclusive contracts that create barriers to entry for competitors. Continually innovate and evolve, making it difficult for others to replicate your success.

Cultivate a Culture of Strategic Agility and Adaptability

The bedrock of long-term success lies in cultivating a culture of strategic agility and adaptability. Foster an environment that encourages curiosity, risk-taking, and continuous learning. Instill a

mindset where failures are seen as opportunities for growth and innovation. Develop mechanisms for swift decision-making and implementation, allowing the organization to pivot when needed. Encourage open communication and feedback loops to ensure alignment with market shifts and customer needs.

Transcending differentiation requires a holistic approach. Understand the market intricacies to pinpoint your unique value proposition, harness disruptive innovations to redefine industry norms, fortify your business with sustainable advantages, and nurture a culture that champions adaptability.

The pursuit of a competitive edge is not merely about setting yourself apart; it is about carving an enduring niche where innovation, resilience, and strategic foresight converge to propel you forward in the ever-evolving marketplace.

Chapter Four

Market Intelligence: Unlock the Secrets of Your Customers

In today's era, bid farewell to the mystique of crystal balls and mystic whispers in market research. Understanding your customers transcends mystical proclamations; it is about cracking the encrypted digital chromosome that defines their online presence. Enter the realm of market intelligence - your gateway to decoding the intricate web of insights that steer their every digital interaction. This shift transforms you from a bewildered bystander to a strategic maestro, harnessing data-driven insights like focused beams of light, illuminating the clandestine desires and motivations steering their clicks, swipes, and purchases.

But this is not a mere display of graphs and figures. It is a profound immersion into the psyche of your audience. It is immersing yourself in their online conversations, discerning the nuanced tones of their social media outbursts, and deciphering the subtle language of their online reviews. It is about transmuting their whispered frustrations in cozy coffee shops into actionable, tangible insights. It is about transcending the surface behavior - going beyond the "what" of their actions to unravel the emotional "why" fueling their every decision-making stride.

In the vast expanse of modern commerce, understanding your customers is the key that unlocks the doors to sustained success. Let us delve into the profound art of deciphering the intricate patterns of consumer behavior and needs.

Master the Art of Customer Research and Understand the Needs, Desires, and Pain Points

Customer research is not just about scratching the surface; it is about a deep dive into the soul of your audience. It involves meticulously unraveling their needs, desires, and the elusive pain points that impel their decisions. Employ qualitative and quantitative methodologies, from surveys to focus groups, to grasp not only what they say they want but also the unspoken cravings driving their choices. Forge an empathetic connection, aligning your offerings to become the solution they yearn for.

Segment the Market and Tailor Your Approach for Different Customer Personas

One size never fits all in the realm of consumers. Segment your market into distinct personas, each with its unique preferences, behaviors, and pain points. Craft tailored approaches and messages that resonate deeply with each segment, speaking directly to their needs and aspirations.

Understand the nuances between demographics, psychographics, and behavioral traits to fine-tune your strategies for maximum impact.

Utilize Data Analytics to Inform Strategic Decision-Making and Optimize Performance

In the era of big data, wielding analytics is not just an advantage; it is a necessity. Data analytics serves as your compass, guiding strategic decision-making. Leverage sophisticated tools to mine insights from consumer behavior patterns, purchase histories, and engagement metrics. Translate these insights into actionable strategies that optimize performance, from refining marketing campaigns to enhancing product features, ensuring every move aligns with the pulse of your customer base.

Becoming adept in market intelligence transcends mere data collection; it is an art of unraveling the enigma of human behavior. It requires weaving a compelling storyline that strikes chords across varied customer segments, fueled by the unerring compass of data-driven insights. Navigating through the intricate maze of consumer needs and behaviors, armed with robust customer research, segmentation strategies, and data analytics, leads to a profound understanding, empathy, and, ultimately, unwavering customer satisfaction.

This journey into market intelligence is akin to exploring the human psyche through data. It is not just about gathering information; it is about deciphering the underlying motivations behind consumer actions. It is about tuning into their unspoken desires, understanding their diverse preferences, and discerning the emotional triggers that drive their decision-making. In this narrative, data is not just numbers and graphs; it is the portal to unlocking the intricate layers of consumer behavior. It is the key to decoding their language, their aspirations, and their implicit needs.

Moreover, market intelligence is a transformative journey where each insight uncovered becomes a puzzle piece in crafting a customer-centric strategy. It is the fusion of scientific precision with creative storytelling, allowing businesses to resonate authentically with their audience. By segmenting markets effectively, understanding nuanced preferences, and leveraging data-driven analytics, organizations can tailor their offerings, messages, and experiences, creating an emotional bond that transcends transactional relationships.

Ultimately, mastering market intelligence is a multifaceted endeavor— it is about not just knowing the 'what' of consumer behavior but delving into the profound 'why.' It is a journey that necessitates not just data interpretation but also the art of empathetic connection, culminating in a holistic understanding that fuels long-term customer satisfaction and loyalty.

Chapter Five

The Art of Effective Marketing and Branding: Your Weapon of Mass Persuasion

Armed with the decoder ring of market intelligence, you now have the raw material to craft the ultimate weapon in your arsenal: marketing and branding. But this is not about blasting your message like a sonic boom, hoping it lands on deaf ears. This is about weaving a spell, a narrative so captivating it draws your audience like moths to a flame. It is about crafting an experience that resonates with their deepest values, ignites their aspirations, and makes them shout your story from the rooftops.

Forget the tired slogans and cookie-cutter campaigns of the past. This is about storytelling on steroids, infused with emotional resonance and laser-targeted messaging. It is about understanding the language your tribe speaks, the visuals that make their hearts skip a beat, and the experiences that solidify their loyalty like an unbreakable oath.

So, buckle up, because we are about to embark on a thrilling journey into the heart of customer psychology and the art of persuasion.

We will explore the tools and techniques that transform brands into beacons in the crowded marketplace, attracting customers like moths to a flame and turning them into loyal advocates who sing your praises to the heavens.

After gathering profound market intelligence and gaining a deep understanding of your audience, it is time to wield a powerful tool: marketing and branding. Yet, this is not about shouting into the void; it is about orchestrating a symphony that strikes a chord with your customers.

Gone are the days of stale sales pitches and uninspired ads. Modern marketing is about storytelling, forging emotional connections. It is about tapping into your audience's values, dreams, and creating experiences that resonate profoundly.

Here is the canvas where your marketing masterpiece unfolds:

Brand Storytelling:

Craft a narrative that embodies your brand's essence and purpose. Invite your audience to not just witness but be part of your story. Make them feel seen and aligned with your brand's values.

Content Marketing:

Offer more than products; provide value. Become a trusted source by educating and entertaining. Share content that enriches their lives, fostering a relationship built on trust and expertise.

Targeted Messaging:

Speak directly to your audience's core. Tailor messages to connect with various customer segments.

Address their concerns and aspirations in a way that deeply resonates with their unique experiences.

Omnichannel Experience:

Craft a consistent brand experience across every touchpoint. Ensure that whether online or in-person, encountering your brand remains seamless, embodying its essence.

Build a community:

Create a sense of belonging around your brand. Initiate conversations, forums, and events that unite customers. Cultivate a community where they feel valued and an integral part of something beyond transactions.

Marketing transcends the transactional realm; it is a narrative woven with emotional threads that tie your brand to the very fabric of your customers' lives.

It is about crafting a journey, a connection that resonates deeply, creating an indelible mark in their experiences.

By seamlessly blending brand storytelling, offering valuable content, delivering targeted messages, and ensuring consistently exceptional experiences, your brand becomes more than just a product or service provider. It evolves into a trusted companion, a guide through the intricacies of their journey.

But it goes beyond that. It is about fostering a community, a space where individuals with shared values and aspirations converge.

It is about cultivating a sense of belonging, where they feel not merely customers but integral members of a collective movement.

This approach does not merely garner sales; it cultivates loyalty and advocacy. It transforms one-time buyers into steadfast supporters, devoted to your brand's cause. It is the alchemy that turns brand-consumer interactions into enduring relationships that withstand time and challenges, evolving and thriving with each passing interaction.

Chapter Six
The Innovation Imperative: Disrupt the Status Quo and Rewrite the Rules

Leave behind the realm of gradual progress; this chapter is a bold leap into the vanguard of innovation—a high-voltage expedition to the frontiers of your industry, where the air buzzes with the energy of groundbreaking ideas. This is not about minor tweaks or operational refinements; we are here to shatter conventions, rewrite norms, and ignite the market with transformative innovations.

Think of Uber obliterating traditional taxis, Airbnb revolutionizing bedrooms into global hubs, and Tesla racing toward the future. These trailblazers epitomize the innovation mandate, daring to envision beyond the familiar and unleashing disruptive forces upon stagnant industry waters.

But how does one cultivate this relentless thirst for disruption, this unyielding hunger for the novel?

Infuse your innovation with audacious experimentation, where creativity flows freely beyond conventional boundaries. Embrace the excitement of failure, engaging in the delicate dance between risk and reward.

Leverage the cutting-edge capabilities of Artificial intelligence, big data, and the Internet of Things as the engine room for your disruptive ventures. These digital realms brew the potions of your innovation alchemy.

Attract and nurture visionaries who see the world through a unique lens. Encourage their curiosity, empower them to envisage beyond limits, and witness their transformation into architects of your future.

Forge collaborative partnerships that break barriers. Join forces with disruptors, startups, and innovators who share your hunger for change. Together, rewrite the industry's rulebook.

Let empathy guide your innovations, resonating deeply with your customers' realities. Listen to their grievances and aspirations, crafting solutions that harmonize with their world.

Remember, innovation is not a one-time affair; it is a continual evolution. The market is ever-changing, and your innovations must be nimble predators in this landscape. Be adaptable, be agile, and forever remain the hungering force for disruptive change.

So, ignite your imagination, fuel the flames of innovation, and brace yourself to unleash this force. This is your opportunity to rewrite the narrative, to become the pioneer whose name echoes as a symbol of audacious brilliance.

Hint!!!

o Qudzy Corporation faced declining market share and fading relevance in an industry ripe with competition, prompting the urgent need for transformative change.

o Embracing the innovation imperative, Qudzy Corporation dismantled traditional barriers, fostering a culture of audacious thinking and risk-taking.

o Strategic investments in innovative technologies like AI, data analytics, and IoT, coupled with collaborations with disruptive startups, fueled the company's radical product overhaul.

o The company's innovative initiatives swiftly bore fruit, disrupting established market segments, elevating market share, and spurring a remarkable surge in customer satisfaction.

o Qudzy Corporation's commitment to innovation not only revitalized their brand but also redefined industry standards, setting a precedent for transformative change across the sector.

In the ever-churning vortex of business, stagnation is death. To thrive, to truly dominate, you must embrace the innovation imperative, a relentless pursuit of the new, the disruptive, the game changing. This is not about tinkering around the edges; it is about shattering the status quo and rewriting the rules of your industry.

Forget the tired mantras of "incremental improvement" and "low-hanging fruit." This is about leapfrogging your competitors, about leaving them gasping in the dust as you blaze a trail into uncharted territory. Think Uber disrupting taxis, Airbnb challenging hotels, Tesla electrifying the automotive landscape. These are the heroes of the innovation imperative, the ones who dared to dream beyond the confines of the familiar.

But how do you cultivate this spirit of innovation, this insatiable hunger for the disruptive? Here are the ingredients you will need:

Foster a culture of experimentation: Encourage your team to take risks, to explore unconventional ideas, to fail fast and learn from their mistakes. Let creativity flow freely, unburdened by the shackles of fear and bureaucracy.

Embrace technology as an ally: Leverage innovative technologies like artificial intelligence, big data, and the Internet of Things to unlock new possibilities and revolutionize your industry.

Be the first to adopt, the first to adapt, the first to harness their power for game-changing solutions.

Invest in human capital: Attract and retain the brightest minds, the enthusiastic innovators who thrive on pushing boundaries. Nurture their curiosity, provide them with the resources they need, and empower them to be effective.

Collaborate with the disruptors: Do not see them as enemies, but as potential partners. Collaborate with startups, universities, and other innovators to cross-pollinate ideas and accelerate your journey towards the future.

Embrace a customer-centric mindset: Innovation should not happen in a vacuum. Listen to your customers, understand their needs, and develop solutions that truly address their pain points. Let their voices guide your innovation engine, ensuring your creations resonate in the real world.

Story .... Story!!!

Once upon a time in the quaint land of Corporateveel, where spreadsheets ruled and coffee was the lifeblood, there existed a company named InnovateD. Now, InnovateD was not your run-of-the-mill corporation.

It was a place where creativity tiptoed in the hallways, occasionally high-fiving innovation at the water cooler.

However, one fateful day, a mysterious case of the "Creativity Crisis" hit InnovateD. Ideas were scarcer than a snowflake in summer, and the office whiteboard remained as blank as a freshly laundered shirt.

The CEO, Sir Theodore Innovation, alarmed by this predicament, summoned his trusty team of Idea Whisperers and Brainstorm Wranglers. They convened in the Ideation Lab, a room pulsating with quirky artwork and enough neon lights to challenge a discotheque.

Enter Professor Sparky, a zany scientist armed with an invention that promised to ignite creativity. He unveiled his creation: the "Creativity-O-Matic 3000," a contraption resembling a mishmash of Dr. Seuss gadgets and a sprinkle of Willy Wonka's whimsy.

With a flourish and a puff of confetti, Professor Sparky pressed the "Activate Creativity" button. The contraption buzzed and whirred, emitting a rainbow of lights. But instead of producing ideas, it just hummed a merry tune and blinked in a rather disco-worthy fashion.

Just when despair started to knock, Martha from Accounting accidentally spilled a cup of rainbow-colored coffee onto the machine. Lo and behold! The Creativity-O-Matic 3000 sputtered, coughed, and burst into a shower of glitter, sprinkling the room with its newfound sparkle.

In the aftermath of this whimsical chaos, something miraculous happened. Ideas surged like a flock of birds in spring. Meetings turned into impromptu poetry slams, and the whiteboard transformed into a canvas of wild doodles.

From that day on, InnovateD realized that creativity was not a switch to flick; it was magic born from unexpected moments, rainbow-colored mishaps, and the freedom to let loose the quirks within.

And so, dear friends, the Creativity-O-Matic 3000 became a glorified disco ball in the office, reminding everyone that sometimes, the spark of creativity ignites not from machines but from the messy, unpredictable, and wonderfully whimsical moments in life.

Chapter Seven
Build High-Performance Teams: From Solo Symphony to Orchestra of Excellence

Forget the cacophony of dysfunctional teams, riddled with discordant egos and clashing cymbals. This chapter is about crafting a symphony of human talent, where individual notes blend into a harmonious masterpiece of performance. We are talking Navy SEALs in perfect unison, Olympic athletes in synchronized grace, a jazz ensemble where improvisation becomes a shared language of excellence.

These are the high-performance teams, the force multipliers that amplify your vision, fuel your momentum, and propel you towards your goals like a rocket with a thousand boosters. They are the secret sauce, the hidden ingredient that transforms innovative ideas into unstoppable realities.

But how do you orchestrate such a symphony, a team that transcends individual limitations and becomes a single, unstoppable force? Here are the conductor's baton essentials:

A discerning ear for talent: Do not settle for mediocrity. Seek individuals who share your melody, your rhythm, your relentless pursuit of excellence. Look for passion, potential, and a willingness to harmonize with the collective score.

A foundation of trust and transparency: Build an environment where open communication is the conductor's baton, where feedback is a shared harmony, and where every note resonates with respect and understanding. Trust is the glue that binds the orchestra together, the invisible thread that weaves individual talents into a unified whole.

Empowering autonomy and ownership: Do not micromanage. Give your team the freedom to improvise, to solo when the moment calls, to take ownership of their parts and make the music their own. Unleash their potential and watch them compose their own verses of brilliance.

A commitment to continuous learning: Music never stops. Invest in your team's growth, provide them with opportunities to refine their skills, and expose them to new instruments of knowledge. Help them stay ahead of the tempo, embrace new rhythms, and keep their melodies fresh and innovative.

Celebrating triumphs and learning from dissonance: No orchestra perfectly plays every time. There will be stumbles, missed notes, and moments of discord. But these are not failures, they are opportunities to refine the score, to adjust the tempo, and to learn to play in harmony through the challenges. Embrace the dissonance, analyze it, and use it to strengthen your collective melody.

Remember, building a high-performance team is an ongoing process, a continuous concerto of refinement and growth. The market is a dynamic audience, and your team must be able to adapt their performance, improvise fresh solutions, and keep the audience captivated by their brilliance.

So, pick up your conductor's baton, open the score of your vision, and prepare to lead your team to a crescendo of excellence. This is your chance to create a symphony of human potential, a testament to the power of collaboration, and a legacy that resonates long after the final note is played.

Are you ready to conduct the orchestra of your dreams?

Your grand vision, your disruptive innovations, your strategic brilliance – they all amount to nothing without the right people by your side. This is where the high-performance team steps onto the stage, a force multiplier that amplifies your efforts, fuels your momentum, and propels you towards your goals.

Forget the dysfunctional teams of the past, riddled with silos, turf wars, and communication breakdowns. This is about a symphony of talent, where individual strengths blend seamlessly into a collective force of unstoppable power. Think of the Navy SEALs, Olympic athletes, or a well-oiled jazz ensemble – these are the paragons of high-performance, where trust, collaboration, and shared purpose drive them to achieve the impossible.

So, how do you build such a team, a unit that transcends individual egos and becomes a single, unstoppable entity? Here are the cornerstones:

Attract the right talent: Do not settle for mediocrity. Seek out individuals who share your vision, your values, and your relentless drive. Look for passion, potential, and a willingness to learn and grow.

Cultivate a culture of trust and transparency: Build an environment where open communication thrives, where feedback is welcomed, and where everyone feels valued and respected. Trust is the bedrock of high-performance, the foundation upon which collaboration and innovation can flourish.

Empower your team: Do not micromanage. Give your team ownership, autonomy, and the decision-making power to navigate their challenges and make their mark. Unleash their potential and watch them soar.

Foster continuous learning and development: Invest in your team's growth. Provide opportunities for training, mentorship, and skill development. Help them stay ahead of the curve, embrace modern technologies, and hone their expertise.

Celebrate successes and learn from failures: No team is perfect. There will be setbacks and stumbles along the way.

Chapter Eight
Operational Excellence: Streamline Your Processes for Success

In the realm of business success, one cornerstone stands tall – **"operational excellence."** It is the craft of orchestrating an organization's inner workings into a symphony of efficiency and success, harmonizing processes and resources with precision and finesse.

Operational excellence is not a mere routine; it is a strategic endeavor that transcends the day-to-day. It is about dissecting, refining, and elevating every facet of an organization's operations to achieve peak performance and competitiveness.

At its heart lies the meticulous identification and optimization of key business processes. This involves an in-depth analysis, identifying inefficiencies, and fine-tuning operations to eliminate bottlenecks. Focusing efforts on critical processes channels resources for maximum impact, ensuring streamlined operations and heightened productivity.

Yet, the pursuit of operational excellence is not solely a manual endeavor. It encompasses harnessing technology and automation's power. By leveraging innovative tools and digital solutions, outdated processes transform into agile, responsive systems.

These interventions not only accelerate workflows but also infuse operations with agility, reducing errors, minimizing manual intervention, and driving cost efficiencies.

However, beyond processes and technology, there is a vital catalyst: a culture of continuous improvement. It is the essence of operational excellence, an environment empowering every team member to contribute to process refinement. This culture values innovation, embraces feedback, and fosters an environment where refining operations becomes ingrained in the organizational ethos.

From supply chain optimization to customer service enhancements and beyond, operational excellence is not a static endpoint; it is an ongoing journey. It is an unwavering commitment to evolving processes, embracing technological advancements, and fostering a culture that champions efficiency and perpetual improvement. Ultimately, operational excellence becomes the cornerstone propelling organizations toward sustained success in a fiercely competitive and ever-evolving marketplace.

In the intricate tapestry of business success, operational excellence emerges as the linchpin.

It is not merely about running the machinery; it is about orchestrating a symphony of processes and systems harmoniously synchronized to propel an organization towards its goals. Let us delve deeper into the layers of this mastery.

Identify and Optimize Key Business Processes for Efficiency and Effectiveness

Operational excellence begins with a meticulous examination of the inner workings of an organization.

It involves dissecting processes, identifying bottlenecks, and discerning areas ripe for improvement. Through detailed analysis and mapping, businesses can streamline workflows, eliminate redundancies, and enhance overall efficiency.

The key lies in recognizing the core processes driving value and focusing resources on optimizing these pivotal areas. Whether it is refining supply chain logistics, improving customer service workflows, or enhancing production methodologies, every optimized process becomes a brick in the foundation of operational excellence.

Utilize Technology and Automation to Streamline Operations and Reduce Costs

Technology stands as the cornerstone in the edifice of operational efficiency. Embracing innovative tools, software, and automation facilitates the transformation of archaic processes into streamlined agile systems.

From sophisticated enterprise resource planning (ERP) systems to task-specific automation, technology not only accelerates processes but also mitigates errors, reduces manual intervention, and drives cost efficiencies. Integrating data-driven decision-making and real-time analytics further empowers organizations to adapt swiftly to dynamic market demands.

Build a Culture of Continuous Improvement and Process Optimization

Operational excellence transcends sporadic enhancements; it embodies an ethos of perpetual advancement. Cultivating a culture of continuous improvement thickens the pursuit of excellence within the organizational DNA.

This cultural shift involves nurturing an environment where every employee contributes to process optimization. Encouraging innovation, valuing feedback, and empowering employees to suggest and implement improvements fosters a sense of ownership and commitment to refining operations.

Regular performance reviews, feedback mechanisms, and dedicated forums for brainstorming and idea-sharing become the crucibles where the spirit of continuous improvement thrives.

In principle, operational excellence is not a destination but a dynamic journey. It is a commitment to refining processes, embracing technological evolution, and nurturing a culture that champions efficiency and constant enhancement. It is the engine that drives businesses toward sustained success in a rapidly evolving marketplace.

Chapter Nine
Cashflow Cadence: Harmonize Your Finances for Success

Welcome to the realm of " Cashflow Cadence: Harmonizing Your Finances for Success," a chapter that unveils the artistry behind wielding financial wisdom to sculpt strategic success. In this intricate tapestry of business prowess, understanding the language of finance is not just about speaking numbers; it is about orchestrating a symphony of fiscal insights to compose a roadmap towards sustainable growth and resilience.

They say understanding financial metrics is akin to deciphering an ancient script—cryptic yet revealing. It is like reading tea leaves, but instead of leaves, you are deciphering balance sheets and income statements. Now, that might not sound as relaxing, but it sure brews a potent potion for informed decision-making!

In the complex ecosystem of business, financial acumen reigns supreme as the guiding beacon. It is not merely about managing funds; it is about wielding financial insights to sculpt strategic decisions that chart the course towards sustainable growth and success.

Understand Key Financial Metrics and the Impact on Strategic Decisions

Financial literacy is the cornerstone of informed decision-making. It entails comprehending crucial metrics like cash flow, profitability ratios, debt-to-equity ratios, and return on investment (ROI). Each metric unveils a facet of an organization's financial health and directly influences strategic choices.

Cash flow, the lifeblood of any business, delineates the inflow and outflow of funds, ensuring liquidity and operational viability. Profitability ratios, such as gross margin and net profit margin, delineate earnings relative to expenses, offering insights into operational efficiency. Debt-to-equity ratios illuminate an organization's leverage and financial risk, guiding decisions on capital structure. ROI measures the efficiency of investments, aiding in resource allocation.

Develop and Implement Sound Financial Strategies for Sustainable Growth

Crafting a robust financial strategy involves aligning financial objectives with overarching business goals. It encompasses prudent budgeting, capital allocation, and revenue forecasting while mitigating risks. A well-crafted financial strategy navigates uncertainties, enabling organizations to seize opportunities and weather economic downturns.

This strategy involves setting realistic financial goals, whether for revenue growth, cost optimization, or market expansion. It also entails effective capital management, balancing short-term needs with long-term investments for sustained growth. Additionally, it involves diversifying revenue streams and optimizing operational efficiency to fortify financial health.

Manage Risk Effectively and Mitigate Potential Financial Challenges

Risk management is the guardian of financial stability.

It is about identifying, assessing, and mitigating potential risks that can undermine financial objectives. These risks span market volatility, regulatory changes, economic downturns, or unforeseen disruptions.

Implementing robust risk management strategies involves diversification of investments, hedging against market fluctuations, and maintaining adequate reserves to cushion against uncertainties. Moreover, it necessitates compliance with regulatory standards, ensuring legal and ethical integrity in financial operations.

Chapter Ten
Leading Through Crisis and Uncertainty: The Art of Adaptation

In the tempestuous arena of modern leadership, the winds of change blow with relentless force. Unforeseen disruptions, market shifts, and unforeseen crises can threaten to capsize even the most resilient vessel. This is the crucible where the art of adaptation, a potent alchemy of resilience and strategic foresight, emerges as the defining mark of effective leadership.

Navigate the Churning Seas of Disruption:

The market, once a predictable ocean, has transformed into a churning sea, where yesterday's charts and compasses offer scant guidance. Modern technologies emerge like rogue waves, consumer preferences shift with the tide, and geopolitical storms can leave entire fleets in ruins. In this dynamic landscape, the leader who clings to outdated strategies courts disaster. Instead, adaptability becomes the lifeblood of survival. Leaders must scan the horizon with the keen eyes of seasoned navigators, constantly anticipating the next squall and pivoting their course with the agility of a seasoned sailor.

Adapt with Strategic Foresight:

But adaptability is not merely a reactive dance. It is a symphony of strategic foresight, where leaders pre-empt the winds of change.

This requires cultivating a culture of scenario planning and risk assessment, where potential disruptions are not mere shadows, but fleshed-out adversaries. By rigorously questioning assumptions and exploring diverse scenarios, leaders can build flexible strategies that bend with the wind, preserving their core vision while adjusting their sails to the ever-shifting currents.

Forge Resilience from the Flames of Failure:

The path of adaptation is seldom smooth. Mistakes will be made, decisions will be miscalculated, and unforeseen shoals will threaten to tear at the hull but in these moments of adversity, the true leader embraces the crucible of failure as an opportunity for growth. By fostering a culture of "fail fast, learn faster," where mistakes are not punished but dissected and utilized, leaders can transform setbacks into potent injections of wisdom. Each misstep becomes a steppingstone, each error a vector correction on the path to a more resilient and prepared future.

Build a Bulwark of Collective Resilience

Leadership in the face of uncertainty is not a solitary endeavor. It is a symphony played by a resilient orchestra, where every member contributes to the collective melody of adaptation. This requires fostering a culture of open communication, where concerns are not silenced but embraced, and feedback flows freely, enriching the decision-making process. By empowering individuals to take ownership and adapt to changing circumstances, leaders can create a decentralized network of resilience, where every member acts as a bulwark against the storm.

Emerge Stronger and More Prepared

Adaptability is not merely a shield against adversity; it is a sword that carves a path to success. By embracing change, learning from setbacks, and fostering a culture of resilience, leaders can transform their organizations into nimble vessels, capable of navigating the treacherous waters of uncertainty and emerging stronger, wiser, and more prepared for the next storm. This is the legacy of the adaptive leader: a thriving organization, a united team, and a testament to the enduring power of human resilience in the face of the unknown.

Adaptation is not a one-stop destination; it is a continuous dance amidst the uncertainty disco ball.

Let us examine how LeloGro, a promising GreenTech startup, navigated the challenges of the global pandemic and emerged stronger.

The Challenge: LeloGro, pioneering sustainable vertical farming technology, faced an unprecedented crisis as COVID-19 disrupted supply chains, halted fundraising, and cast doubt on the future of green ventures. Their innovative urban farms, reliant on fresh produce delivery, suddenly faced limited customer access and a volatile market.

The Leader's Response: Sarah, LeloGro's founder and CEO, embraced the "Art of Adaptation." She demonstrated the following key leadership qualities:

Calm and Decisive: Sarah instilled confidence in her team by presenting a clear understanding of the crisis while acknowledging the inherent uncertainty. She made quick, decisive decisions to adapt operations, prioritizing employee safety and customer service.

Transparency and Communication: Sarah maintained open communication with her team, investors, and customers. She shared updates regularly, fostering a sense of unity and shared purpose in navigating the turbulent landscape.

Agility and Innovation: Sarah pivoted LeloGro's focus, recognizing the increased demand for local, sustainable food sources.

They partnered with local grocery stores and restaurants, offering contactless delivery and subscription services. Additionally, they shifted resources to develop and market a home-based vertical farming kit for individual customers.

Empathy and Resilience: Sarah recognized the emotional toll of the crisis on her team and prioritized their well-being. She offered flexible work arrangements, mental health support, and encouraged open communication of challenges. This built trust and strengthened team spirit.

Outcomes and Impact:

Increased Revenue: Despite initial setbacks, LeloGro's rapid adaptation and focus on local food security led to a 30% increase in revenue within 6 months. Their home-based kits became a surprise hit, expanding their customer base and creating a new revenue stream.

Enhanced Brand Image: LeloGro's initiative-taking response to the crisis garnered positive media attention, portraying them as a responsible and innovative company. This strengthened their brand image and attracted new investors.

Stronger Team and Culture: Sarah's leadership fostered a resilient and adaptable team, capable of quickly pivoting and facing future challenges with confidence. LeloGro emerged from the crisis with a stronger internal culture and a renewed sense of purpose.

Lessons Learned:

Calm and decisive leadership is critical in crisis situations. Clear communication, transparency, and quick decision-making instill confidence and empower teams to navigate turbulent times.

Agility and innovation are key to overcoming disruption. Leaders must be prepared to pivot strategies, embrace new opportunities, and adapt to rapidly changing circumstances.

Empathy and resilience are essential for team well-being. Prioritizing employee well-being fosters a supportive environment, strengthens team spirit, and enhances long-term success.

LeloGro's story highlights the vital role of strong leadership in leading organizations through crisis and uncertainty. By embodying the principles of calm decisiveness, transparent communication, agile adaptation, and empathetic resilience, Sarah steered LeloGro to not only survive, but thrive in the face of an unforeseen challenge. This case study highlights the importance of these leadership qualities for any organization preparing to navigate an unpredictable future.

Further Discussion:

- **How can leaders balance the need for decisive action with the importance of gathering information and considering options during a crisis?**
- **What are some effective strategies for fostering team adaptability and innovation in an uncertain environment?**
- **How can leaders cultivate and maintain resilience in themselves and their teams to navigate prolonged periods of uncertainty?**

This case study prompts deeper exploration of crisis leadership and its vital role in organizational success. By analyzing LeloGro's journey, we gain valuable insights applicable to navigating the ever-changing business landscape.

Chapter Eleven
Build a Sustainable Enterprise: Beyond Profits and Growth

The siren song of profits has long lured businesses towards a singular goal: relentless growth. But in the face of a dawning environmental crisis and mounting social inequalities, this melody rings hollow. Today, a new chorus rises, demanding a different dance – one where sustainability takes center stage, weaving a harmonious tapestry of environmental, social, and governance (ESG) principles into the fabric of every business decision.

Beyond the Profit Motive

Building a sustainable enterprise is not about sacrificing profits; it is about redefining what success truly means. It is about recognizing that short-term gains that come at the cost of environmental degradation or societal harm are pyrrhic victories. By integrating ESG principles into your strategic framework, you shift your focus from the fleeting flicker of quarterly reports to the long-term well-being of your planet, your people, and your community.

Weaving the Threads of ESG

ESG is not a bolt-on accessory; it is the very warp and weft of your business. Here is how to weave its threads into your operations:

Environmental Stewardship: Embrace renewable energy, reduce waste, and minimize your carbon footprint. Be a guardian of the planet, not a plunderer.

Social Responsibility: Invest in your employees, foster diversity and inclusion, and champion fair labor practices. Be a catalyst for positive change, not a perpetuator of inequality.

Governance Integrity: Uphold ethical standards, ensure transparency in your operations, and hold yourself accountable to stakeholders. Be a beacon of trust, not a shadow of deceit.

Balancing the Scales of Impact

Sustainable business is not about choosing between profits and principles; it is about finding the sweet spot where both can thrive. By optimizing your operations for efficiency, innovating for environmental solutions, and building trust with your customers, you unlock the potential for shared prosperity, where financial success fuels positive impact.

Building a Legacy of Purpose

In a world increasingly defined by short-term thinking and fleeting trends, building a sustainable enterprise is about leaving a legacy of purpose. It is about creating a company that does not just exist to generate profits, but to make a positive difference in the world. It is about inspiring future generations to dance to a different rhythm, where success is measured not just by the bottom line, but by the handprint we leave on the world.

The journey towards sustainability is not without its challenges, but the rewards are immeasurable. By embracing ESG principles, you position your company as a leader in a changing world, attracting talent, fostering loyalty, and securing long-term growth. So, silence the siren song of short-term gains and join the chorus of change. Weave sustainability into your business, and watch as your enterprise not only thrives, but makes a lasting impact on the world around you.

Are you ready to redefine success? Then step onto the stage of sustainability, embrace the ESG principles, and embark on a journey towards a future where profit and purpose dance in perfect harmony.

Chapter Twelve
The Indelible Leader: Build a Winning Legacy

Leadership is not a title etched in glass; it is a masterpiece carved in the hearts and minds of those you inspire. The truly indelible leader is not merely a captain steering a ship, but a sculptor, molding the potential of their team into a legacy that transcends time and circumstance. This is the journey of building a leadership that leaves its mark, not just on profits and balance sheets, but on the very fabric of your industry and the world.

Forging the Qualities of Indelible Leadership

Leadership is not a singular diamond, but a multifaceted gem, each facet reflecting a different essential quality:

Vision with a View: Indelible leaders are not passengers on the current; they are navigators, charting a course towards a horizon unseen by others. They envision a future both ambitious and attainable, painting a canvas that ignites the imagination of their team.

Courage in the Face of Uncertainty: The path to success is rarely a smooth one. Indelible leaders are not deterred by the inevitable storms; they face them head-on with unwavering courage, inspiring their team to weather any challenge and emerge stronger.

Integrity as a Guiding Light: Trust is the cornerstone of any legacy. Indelible leaders walk the talk, upholding the highest ethical standards, and leading by example, ensuring their actions resonate with authenticity and integrity.

Empathy as the Bridge of Connection: Great leaders understand that success is not a solo endeavor. They cultivate an environment of empathy, fostering genuine connections with their team, and recognizing that every individual plays a vital role in the collective journey.

Growth as the Unending Pursuit: Leaders who stand still become monuments to the past. Indelible leaders are perpetual learners, constantly seeking new knowledge, embracing innovation, and encouraging their team to do the same, keeping the fire of growth burning bright.

Inspiring the Symphony of Potential

Leadership is not about dictating; it is about conducting. Indelible leaders know that every member of their team holds a unique instrument, and it is their job to draw out the harmony within.

They:

Empower individuals to find their voice: Micromanagement stifles creativity. Indelible leaders provide their team with the autonomy and resources to explore their potential, fostering a culture of ownership and initiative.

Celebrate individual strengths and contributions: Every note matters in the symphony. Indelible leaders recognize and celebrate the diverse talents of their team, weaving them together into a tapestry of brilliance.

Champion learning and development: Growth is not a destination; it is a continuous journey. Indelible leaders invest in the development of their team, providing opportunities for learning and personal growth, ensuring their skills remain vibrant and their potential ever evolving.

Foster collaboration and communication: Silos are the enemies of progress. Indelible leaders break down barriers, encourage open communication, and nurture a spirit of collaboration, where ideas and perspectives flow freely, fueling innovation and collective success.

Leaving a Legacy that Echoes Through Time

The mark of an indelible leader is not their own success, but the impact they have on the world around them.

They:

Champion ethical and sustainable practices: Indelible leaders understand that their actions have far-reaching consequences. They embed ethical and sustainable principles into the core of their business, leaving a legacy that benefits not just their company, but the planet and its inhabitants.

Give back to the community: Indelible leaders recognize their responsibility to the communities they serve. They dedicate resources and time to causes that matter, leaving a lasting positive impact on the lives of others.

Inspire future generations of leaders: Indelible leaders are not islands; they are lighthouses. They mentor and guide others, sharing their knowledge and experience, ensuring the torch of leadership is passed on to capable hands.

Building an indelible legacy is not a sprint; it is a marathon. It requires unwavering commitment, continuous learning, and a deep-seated belief in the power of human potential. But the rewards are immeasurable. It is about creating a legacy that resonates beyond profits and market share, a legacy that echoes in the hearts and minds of those you lead, a legacy that leaves the world a better place than you found it.

Conclusion

Strategize, Execute, and Dominate is your Blueprint for Business Mastery

We have sailed through the intricate landscape of business strategy, dissecting its essential elements, and equipping ourselves with the tools to dominate the competitive arena. Now, as we stand at the precipice of action, let us distill the key takeaways and ignite the fire of implementation:

The Transformative Power of Strategic Thinking

Debunk the myths, embrace the imperative: Strategy is not a crystal ball; it is a compass, guiding you from mere survival to thriving in the ever-shifting business landscape.

Craft your winning formula: Align your vision, mission, and values with market realities, and let SWOT analysis illuminate your path. Set SMART goals, measure your progress, and watch your ambition materialize.

Unleash your competitive edge: Dive into the depths of your market, unearth your unique value proposition, and build a moat around your business with disruptive innovation and strategic agility.

From Vision to Execution: The Tactical Toolkit:

Unlock the secrets of your customers: Master the art of market intelligence, segment your audience, and let data be your crystal ball, revealing their desires and pain points.

Craft a brand story that resonates: Weave a compelling narrative that captures hearts and minds and let your marketing campaigns be brushstrokes painting your brand identity across channels.

Build your high-performance engine: Attract talent that fuels your vision, foster collaboration, empower ownership, and watch your team transform into a force of strategic execution.

Navigating the Battlefield: Executing with Excellence

Streamline your processes for success: Identify and optimize, utilize technology to your advantage, and embrace continuous improvement, transforming every dollar into a driver of growth.

Make every dollar count: Become fluent in the language of finance, develop sound financial strategies, manage risk effectively, and watch your business soar to new heights.

Lead through the storm: Embrace resilience and foresight, adapt your strategy with agility in the face of uncertainty, and learn from setbacks to emerge stronger and wiser.

Dominating the Future: Sustainable Growth and Innovation:

Ignite the engine of innovation: Cultivate a culture that champions experimentation, embrace disruptive trends, nurture ideas, and watch them blossom into game-changing products and services.

Beyond profits, towards purpose: Integrate ESG principles into your core, leave a legacy of positive impact, and build a business that thrives on a foundation of responsibility and ethical leadership.

Sculpt your indelible legacy: Foster the qualities of the successful leader, inspire your team, and leave a lasting mark on the world, one strategic action at a time.

This book is not just a passive journey; it is a call to action. Grab your strategic toolkit, wield the power of your newfound knowledge, and embark on the path to dominating your future. Remember, the world awaits your masterpiece. So, strategize, execute, and dominate!

References

Drucker, P. F. (1994). Disrupting business: What great strategists teach us about competing in the age of disruption. Harper Business.

Harvard Business Review. (2018). HBR guide to thinking strategically. Harvard Business Review Press.

Kelley, T., & Kelley, D. (2001). The art of innovation: Lessons in creativity from IDEO, America's leading design firm. Doubleday.

Moore, G. A. (1991). Crossing the chasm: Marketing and selling high-tech products to mainstream customers. HarperCollins Publishers.

Porter, M. E. (1998). Competing for advantage: Creating and sustaining competitive advantage. Free Press.

Drucker, P. F. (2006). Customer centricity: How to put the customer at the heart of everything you do. Harvard Business Review Press.

Davenport, T. H., & Harris, J. G. (2007). Competing in analytics: The new science of winning. Harvard Business School Press.

Mackay, H. (1997). The customer is always right (and other essential rules for running a business). HarperCollins Publishers.

Miller, D. (2017). Building a story Brand: Clarify your message, connect with customers, and grow your business. HarperCollins Publishers.

Jones, J. P. (2003). Branding: In five and a half pieces. John Wiley & Sons.

Lencioni, P. (2002). The five dysfunctions of a team: A leadership fable. Jossey-Bass.

Ries, E. (2011). The lean startup: How today's entrepreneurs use continuous innovation to create radically successful businesses. Crown Business.

Dweck, C. S. (2006). Mindset: The new psychology of success. Ballantine Books.

Heifetz, R. E., Linsky, M., & Donald, K. D. (2009). Leading through crisis: How to build resilience in yourself and your organization. Harvard Business Review Press.

Pink, D. H. (2020). Disrupting ideas: How businesses can adapt and thrive in a volatile world. Riverhead Books.

Michalko, M. (2006). Thinkertoys: A handbook of creative-thinking techniques. New World Library.

Osterwalder, A., & Pigneur, Y. (2017). Sustainable value creation: Strategies for business success in a changing world. John Wiley & Sons.

Polman, P., Winston, A., & Esty, D. C. (2015). Business for good: The role of business in a changing world. Harvard Business Review Press.

About the Author

Adedayo Adetokun is a highly accomplished corporate strategy specialist and strategic human resource management professional with over a decade of diversified expertise. He possesses a wealth of experience in crafting and implementing strategies, overseeing management and organizational development, and spearheading projects.

Presently, Adedayo holds a pivotal leadership position as the head of Business Advisory in a prominent Consulting Company. In this role, she orchestrates the formulation, execution, and assessment of strategic initiatives that drive business success. His unparalleled skills in strategy development and evaluation have solidified her position as a leader in the field. Contact Adedayo via Adedayo.mutiu@yandex.com.